When I was Young

poems by

Dorthy Knouse Koepke

To my dear Luther clan,

— My mother's book.

Judy Koepke
Spring 2012

Previously Published Books

Close to My Heart
Love Made Me Do It

Copyright 2011 by Dorthy Knouse Koepke, Norfolk, Nebraska
All rights reserved.

Book design and layout by Lana Koepke Johnson,
Koepke Design, Lincoln, Nebraska

LIBRARY OF CONGRESS CATALOGING-IN-PUBLICATION DATA
Koepke, Dorthy Knouse
When I Was Young by Dorthy Knouse Koepke
ISBN: 978-0-557-91620-7

FIRST EDITION

for my late husband Herman,
who gave a lifetime of encouragement and adoration for my writing

for my children,
Judy, Janis, JoAnn, Galen, Gary, Gene, Lonnie, Lana, Lynne and Jeffrey,
their spouses,
and my many, amazingly talented, grandchildren,
who provided me with endless material and inspiration

for all my dear friends and relatives,
who also gave me inspiration and encouragement
to record my life and improve my writing

Foreword

I first met Dorthy Koepke at a statewide meeting of the Chaparral Poets, and over the years I have come to know her work fairly well. In fact, I am confident that I could pick out from a sheaf of poems the titles that were hers. Like all good poets, her voice is distinctly her own.

The first characteristic of that voice is its directness of vision, its honesty. In "April Concert," for example, the poet laments a development that threatens the habitat of some frogs that make their home at the edge of a nearby pond; here the creatures go on with their lives and their springtime songs watched over by the inaccessible nature of moon and stars and night-time thunderstorms. The poet hopes that the developer is aware of this, knowing, as she herself does, that development engenders its own mindless momentum. "Cat Scan" begins with an observation like a journal entry: "Pain At The Intersection Of Seven Scars..." In "Fending Off Aging" (a title which seems to parody current ads for facial creams and other beauty aids), Dorthy, noting her lapses of memory, says

> names often fail me,
> by the time I remember
> who I am talking to, I forget
> what I wanted to say.

A second characteristic of Dorthy's verse is also reflected in this passage, and that is its humor. One winces momentarily at the aptness of the lines above, then smiles at their winsome humor. Similarly, in "What Does It Matter," a poem set at a funeral service, the poet weighs the relative unimportance of a run in her hose against the somber thoughts of the occasion, and somehow this juxtaposition both amuses and comforts.

A third important characteristic is the poet's profound love of and respect for children. "A Walk With Elizabeth" wonderfully captures these qualities. Seldom has a child's free-wheeling imagination been so movingly presented. This poem seems the masterpiece of the present collection.

Lastly, and more generally, is the delight one gleans from some of the poet's own delight in the rich resources of language. Take "Country Church," for instance. Some of its lines turn the image into metaphor, as in "an embrace of pines" and "hackberry leaves/sing praises like a soft sweep of angels..." This is good, very good. But don't take my word for it. Get into the poems and make up your own list of favorites.

Roy Scheele
Associate Professor of English
Poet in Residence
Doane College
Crete, Nebraska

Contents

I. Life

When I Was Young 2

Life 3

Waiting For The Stork 4

Prolific Mother 6

Farewell 7

Redeem The Time 9

Fending Off Aging 10

Can't Wait 12

Cat Scan 13

Finale 15

The Shredders 16

Blood Transfusion 17

Bedtime Blues 19

April Concert 20

Aftermath 22

The Cure 23

Waiting For The Doc 24

Vioxx 25

When Does It Matter 26

Country Church 27

II. Family

To All My Grandchildren 30
Grandma And Me, Miranda 31
My Basement Visitors 32
The Hugabug 33
Baby And Old Age 34
A Walk With Elizabeth 35
A Louse For Every Hair 38
Saturday Night 39
Our Family Car 40
Trials Of The Firstborn (in 1944) 41
The Hair Rebellion 43
British Columbia Hitchhiker 45
Corned Sausage 46
My Blacksmith Hubby 47
Death In The Nursing Home 48

III. Seasons

The Seasons 50
My Heartstrings Are Tied To The Prairie 51
The Emissaries 52
Summer's Song 53
Morning Meditations 54
Metamorphosis 55

Norfolk	58
Thanksgiving	60
Country	61
The Unveiling	62
A Matter Of Necessity	63
Gasless Get-About	64
The Tree Trimmers	65
The Robin And The Worm	66
Daffodils In Winter	67
Before The Roses Bloom	68
Autumn Leaves	69
Go, Go Little Birds	70
The Believers	71
Little Green Apples	72
Fisherman's Delight	73
Roz And Rosy	74
Silly Milly's Escapade	75
Little Mouse In My House	77
Renaissance Romance	78
One Question, Please	79
Mistaken Calendar	80
Line Dance	81
Prairie Song	82
The Prairie Pines	84

Victory	85
When Death Comes	86
Life's Setting Sun	87
Meditation	88
When The Master Calls	89
Plea Bargain	90

I. Life

When I Was Young

When I was young,
I expected to be
a distinguished author at thirty.
I tried,
but dirty dishes sprouted
in kitchen sinks like radish seeds
tossed on fertile soil after rain.
I wrote my life on burping babies
and pre-disposable diapers,
harmonized with the twang
of milk rivers in tin pails
and the chop-chop of hoe
on weeds in the garden.
I wrote on the minds of children
all that I knew to be good,
page after page, stumbling sometimes,
wishing the script could be rewritten,
knowing the seeds for the stories
will go on forever.
Perhaps I am a distinguished author.

Life

Youth, vibrant youth,
with restless impatience
seeking immediate fulfilment,
trying to do everything
all at once,
using as appetizers
the experiences it takes
a lifetime to savor.

Age, reflecting,
finds life somewhat akin
to playing the tuba.
Players who insist
on releasing their breath
all at once have none
remaining for the crucial
moment when the band
actually starts playing.

Waiting For The Stork

I have the strangest feeling,
something must be wrong,
I went to see the doctor,
Heavens!! Two whole months along.

Pa in his elation,
can scarce control his joy,
already he can picture,
a manly little boy.

I heave-ho after eating,
I'm dizzy as a duck,
I hate the smell of cooking,
and I'm losing all my pluck.

I read the latest books,
on baby's proper care,
they sound so complicated,
I'm drowning in despair.

I've never been so sleepy,
since I was two days old,
I'm tired as the dickens,
and I shiver in the cold.

Hubby's feeling lonesome,
he has to eat alone,
while I occupy the daybed,
and gag and think and groan.

My stomach is expanding,
I'm looking like a sack,
sagging in the front,
and swaying in the back.

My eyes and tongue pop out,
when I must stoop or bend,
and all the clothes I have,
just reach around one end.

My legs are tight and swollen,
I lie awake at night,
while Hubby snores beside me,
now I don't think that's right.

My back has got a toothache,
I'm sure I weigh a ton,
I'm almost dead from waiting,
while Junior's getting done.

Junior's so rambunctious,
he'll wear my stomach out,
I've never been so - heavens!
Is this what love's about?

Prolific Mother

The whole world condemns me
they speak of me with shame
a prostitute has more honor
for prolific mother is my name.

For all the world's problems
they judge me to blame
for hunger, for earth's pollution
for the extinction of wild game.

What should I do with my treasures
my unwarranted ten
wind them backwards like
an old movie? What then?

Farewell

Sixty years of memories,
since our wedding vows,
are what you left me now
to heal my grief.
Sixty years, it sounds so long
yet seems so brief.

Sixty years of memories
written on our minds,
wasted lines of arguments
with forgiveness intertwined,
inspired devotion that withstood
the stress of bad times with the good.

Blessed with joy of children,
doctor bills and sleepless nights,
Sunday school and church bell chimes,
wavy locks turned bald and white,
through it all love was the glue
that bound the pages tight.

I was with you when you left me,
in my mind I bid you go,
but my heart cried, "Await a while,
once more let me say, 'I love you,'
and watch your face light up with smiles."

Now you lie here cold as marble,
vacant house of departed soul,
yet I know you sing in heaven,
praising God in promised mansions
singing praises that you practiced
working hard in barn and field,
locking cows in row of stanchions
bringing in the harvest yields.

Farewell, my dear, I too am singing,
living out life's final stages,
writing memory's ending pages
praising God in word and song,
knowing that I soon will see you,
knowing that I won't be long.

Redeem the Time

Was it only yesterday
that I was born,
thrust into the coldness
of unpreparedness,
into the hands of a
convenient neighbor,
who untangled the birth cord
and released the blood
to my blue lips?

Yes, we all ask it,
where have the years gone?
We have no answer.
Like a passenger come late
to the airport, we ask it,
where has the plane gone,
while I was packing
my belongings?

And I ask it, too,
and I wonder,
what have I done with them,
the days, the hours gone by?

Now I will make reservations
for the rest of the journey more wisely,
and savor the small things,
forgetting myself and easing the heartache
and giving hope to the hopeless,
sharing my faith with the faithless,
and showing love to the unloved.

Still serving, yet wisely prepared
and waiting at the gate
for my Pilot to announce
that my plane is ready for boarding.

Fending Off Aging

Medical news letters,
books, any supplemental
research on physical and mental
functions of aging populations,
are my forte.

Research recommends:
work your body to the max,
trot up mountains, hike and bike,
hop around the dance floor
to lively music, waltz or polka,
any get-movin' action that hustles
the heartbeat; keep your body
receptive to positive activity.

Same for the brain:
work it to the max,
play chess, pinochle,
take a class, be creative,
compete with young brains,
learn to foil a computer virus;
keep working brain cells
receptive to positive activity.

My body, at eighty-five,
like my aging Cadillac,
needs regular maintenance;
it creaks, needs frequent lubrication,
transmission growls, gears grind,
battery needs charging,
radiator leaks, seats sag.
Still, I work it to the max.

My brain, well, it is a hassle.
Names often fail me;
by the time I remember
who I am talking to, I forget
what I wanted to say. No fret,
my medical newsletters relay
the consensus that this frustration
is normal for aging baby boomers;
I am confident this also applies to me,
although I have already boomed.

Can't Wait

Come early, don't be late,
Then there's time to meditate;
How can I, my stomach growls,
Away with consonants and vowels,
My creativity can wait,
I want my chicken-fried steak!

Cat Scan

Pain at the intersection of seven scars,
crisscrossing my abdominal map,
prompted my surgeon to order
a cat scan the very next day.

Like cat eyes seeing images in the dark,
the cat scan copies the contours
of my innards, slice by slice,
as if I were a diaphanous piece of cheese.

With automatic precision, though sympathetic,
duty-bound, the nurse sends me home
with necessary supplies to prepare
my body for this diagnostic event.

Two packets of fake milk shakes
spiked with some nauseous flavoring,
progeny of laundry starch we used to cook,
to prime white shirts for ironing.

To be downed tonight at thirty past nine,
and thirty past eight in the morning;
like Cinderella's ball, food stops at midnight,
with caffeine forbidden the whole long day.

Like a well-trained puppy, I followed orders,
drank the drinks, spurned the coffee pot,
arrived at the hospital, checked into x-ray,
inwardly winced at the IV needle.

Directed down the hall to the x-ray room,
I spied the pitcher on the receptionist's desk,
yellow-green, it looked like anti-freeze, or worse;
my innards churned, she handed me a glass.

It wasn't lemonade, but I downed the full quart.
The technician claimed me and took me back,
she got me fixed on this curved hard board,
started the IV with some kind of dye.

I overheated like a car on the 4th of July;
the machine started up, slow through the ring.
"Take a deep breath, hold it," said a man's gruff voice.
Breathing, not breathing, I obeyed his firm commands.

Having survived the procedures for that ten-minute ride,
I crawled gratefully off that hard curved bed;
my body, laced through with nauseating brews,
needed coffee, and prayers, that this be my very last scan.

Finale

Precisely
the surgeon's knife
severs the last hold
on motherhood.

But the severing
brings no regrets
or tears
that conception
and birth
are lost forever.

The nest overflows
the heart already
has brimmed over
and this tired body
is content to function
as grandmother.

The Shredders

The paper shredder waits beside my chair,
hungry as a monster breaking fast,
waiting to devour all paper evidence
of a life that has mostly passed.

From my mind's file of memories,
I see a vision from long ago,
of my farmer shredding fields of corn
into waiting wagons, row after row,
filling high the empty silo,
feed for his steers on wintry days.

My farmer's shredder worked to sustain life
mine shreds evidence of life away.
Now his shredder sits in another's shed;
another's corn grows in his fields.
When morning breaks, its appetite intense,
my shredder hungers for documents,
as my farmer's once did for his corn.

Though I feel my time could be better spent,
I sit here shredding papers,
some tattered and filmy with dust.
Sacks and stacks, a sixty-year blend,
sliced into unreadable ribbons,
our life from beginning to end.

Filling black bags for my garbage man,
sparing my children the tedious task,
of sorting the trash from the treasures.
On lonely nights, with my head on his pillow,
I lie awake in the street light's glow,
and ponder the universal question:
where did our precious years go?

Blood Transfusion

Drip,
drip,
precious wine of life,
a gift
from a stranger's well
of blood.

Drop by slow drop
mingle
cell with cell,
and raise
this weak body up
from the grasp
of the grave.

Down,
down,
from the unit
hung high,
metronome steady,
life seeps,
ruby red,
through the needle,
and satisfies
the thirsty vein.

Reprieved,
for a time
by mortal blood,
I cling, new visioned,
to the greater miracle
of Christ's precious blood,
and the ultimate gift
of eternal life.

I rest,
cross-matched by faith,
to my Savior's
Blood Bank.

Bedtime Blues

Five of us kids slept in one bed,
Two at the foot, three at the head,
There was not a night we could forget,
For every morn the bed was wet.

If you slept at the head,
They washed your feet
If you slept at the foot,
They wet your seat.

The middle sagged a foot or more,
All night long we touched the floor,
Sleeping was a dreadful trial,
Five kids lying in a pile.

Five kids lying in one place,
Each with an elbow in his face,
Somebody's foot against your nose,
Somebody raining on your toes,
Somebody's knee against your neck,
While your stomach got a kick.

We hated to think the day was done,
And rejoiced at the rising sun,
For it surely wasn't any fun,
To sleep in that aquarium!

April Concert

It is April,
peek-a-boo stars
and sliver of moon,
fence with billowing thunderheads
in the electric night sky.

In the parking lot
at Pic-N-Save,
I stow my groceries
in the maw of Caddie trunk,
and pause to listen
to frogs singing
far beyond the skeletons
of buildings rising,
quick as overnight toadstools,
in the new development
scarring yonder meadow.

I slam the trunk shut
as cloud mountains,
dark and rumbling,
vanquish the light of moon and star;
lightening fingers trace patterns
through the blackness,
vibrate my paved world
with slaps of thunder,
as raindrops splat murky streams
across my dusty windshield.

I aim my Caddie down
Square Turn Boulevard,
pondering the decisions
of the developer,
whose money-eye eagers
to flatten sky-tickling cottonwoods
and feathery willows, that lace

the shore of the placid pond
in yonder green meadow,
where the frogs dwell.
I pray he will remember
that God intended
for frogs to sing
when it is April.

Aftermath

The first blast of winter is over,
arthritic aches rode south on the north wind,
now I am able to climb the steps out of the cellar,
where winter locked the door on happy moods,
and find myself uncontrollably quite delirious.

I want to kick the brace off my leg,
and flit and trill like an uncaged canary
half-flying, hippity-hopping down the street,
a brief bliss of freedom before duty calls.

Prudence cannot completely spoil the spin
of spontaneity - though outwardly a model of tranquility -
diligently cooking a pot of chicken noodle soup,
inwardly, I am having so much fantastic fun.

The Cure

I get a clever inspiration,
To organize a delegation,
To search the corners of creation,
To find a cure for constipation.
When we were wet with perspiration,
We stopped to see my worst relation,
And found a cure for constipation.
I'm not supposed to let it out,
But it was just some sauerkraut.

Waiting For The Doc

I'm sitting in the waiting room,
Looking at the clock,
Sitting there in worry,
Waiting to see the Doc.

I'm thumbing through a magazine,
Shaking in my feet,
Aching in my bottom,
Growing to my seat.

I'm startled out of thinking,
Feeling faint with shock,
At hearing Nurse announce
That I can see the Doc.

Vioxx

Vioxx
oh, oh, my Vioxx,
in a bottle or in a box,
soothed my aches,
soothed my pain,
made me feel
so young again.
Now the FDA
took it away,
and I am left
with creaky bones,
stiffened joints
and daily groan.
I try to sway
the FDA
to let me have
my Vioxx,
in a bottle or in a box.

What Does It Matter

I attended a funeral, unaware
A cob-webby run was snaking its way
Full-length the back of my hose.
I really don't mind if anyone knows.
What does it matter,
Who cares, who cares?

What does it matter, that irrelevant run,
When a teenage driver lost control,
And crashed his car on a highline pole,
And there amid the shattered glass,
The crumpled steel, death made a pass,
And freed his young friend's soul?

What does it matter, that irrelevant run,
When, beside his coffin, loved ones weep,
For the boy that death would not let them keep,
When kisses of sorrow brush lips grown cold,
And arms and eyes ache to enfold
More memories for tomorrow.

Yes, I attended a funeral today,
With a spider-web run spinning its way,
Full-length the back of my hose,
I really don't mind that everyone knows,
For what does it matter?
Who cares, who cares?

Country Church

From our farmhouse upstairs' windows,
forty years our gaze beamed above the cedar
bordered shelter belt to this cross-spired
focal point in the wide sweep of country,
daily renewed, until we retired to the city.

Now our spirits feast on church bells sounding
carillon two blocks away, the congregation's
gift to us, while through the open window, mourning
doves beckon us to stroll through their cemetery,
where an embrace of pines guards its quietness.

My husband and I worship there, sometimes.
Most Sunday mornings we head for country.
We mark the way with fields of corn,
and velvet spread of alfalfa, watch fresh-dropped
calves wobble erect in hilly pastures and
nuzzle for milk, love-licked by protective mothers.

We slow for duck families Sunday-strolling across
roadways, quacking to ponds and water-logged ditches,
while quarter horse mares chew grass breakfasts,
and colts buck and run, tails switching.

We claim our parking stall, grass cushioned.
It is early, seated front row in God's theater,
we listen, breezes brush our faces, hackberry leaves
sing praises like a soft sweep of angels,
cow bellows, somewhere, blend with churn of tractor,
bees hum past car windows.

Rabbits on cotton-ball feet hop beside the church,
meadowlarks welcome us from adjacent meadows,
cock pheasants cackle in the cemetery, the cemetery
inhabited by those we knew well, those we shed tears for,
baked funeral lunch cakes for, decorate graves for.

Our weary bones rebel at driving these
fifteen miles to where the cross-spired country church,
white against the sun, claims the highest country hill.
Yet we come, Sunday after Sunday, like a pair of snow geese
returning to our nesting site, seeking nourishment
to strengthen our wings for the final flight home.

II. Family

To All My Grandchildren

The grasp of tiny fingers,
the all new touch-me-tender-skins,
so natural, yet uniquely rare,
the dark eyes' wondered depth,
the curve of chin,
the downy fluff of hair,
fine spun
from gentle glow of sunrise.
The dear Lord wisely chose
selective genes,
creating out of gracious love,
these tiny ones
to be adored.

Now bless them , Lord,
all my grandchildren,
be their Savior as they grow,
guide their feet on life's pathway,
and day by day
be near to them,
wherever they may go.

Grandma And Me, Miranda

Grandma and me, Miranda,
laughing as we play,
Grandma and me, Miranda,
having fun all day.
Pretending we are the maple tree
waving as it sways,
Pretending we are the branches high
blowing every way,
Pretending we are the golden leaves
whirling all around,
Pretending we are the maple leaves
  falling
    to the
      ground!

My Basement Visitors

My grandchildren are scattered
across my basement in spectacular
gymnastic stance, arms of lilac

laced turtle-neck sweaters crumple
and necks scrunch over backs of
collapsed recliners, faded blue

jeans frolic in corkscrew sprawls on
the floor, hems touching purple
socks dancing tiptoe over the edge

of the toppled green tractor, fuzzy
slippers flip bunny ears in awesome
antics and the I Love

Grandma T-shirt curls sleeping under
the rocker. A fluorescent jacket with
arms outstretched hugs

a zigzag of crayons, and the
stethoscope monitors the headless
Barbie doll clinging to the barn

roof next to a flying cow. Yes, my
grandchildren still inhabit my
basement after their bodies were

snatched by an urgent appointment
arriving too soon, before they could
remove the evidence
of their presence.

The Huga Bug

I am a snuggly Huga Bug,
I specialize in loving hugs,
On days when you are feeling blue,
I am the person near to you,
Who gives at least ten hugs a day,
And sends you happy on your way.
It is such fun to share a hug
And be a snuggly Huga Bug.

Please be a snuggly Huga Bug,
Just give someone a loving hug,
Grandpa, Grandma, father, mother,
Gloomy friends or sister, brother.
Give at least ten hugs a day,
And send them happy on their way.
It is such fun to share a hug,
and be a snuggly Huga Bug.

Baby And Old Age

Babies and Grandma's
follow the same pattern,
in reverse, Babies progress,
increasing skills, Grandma quits
climbing hills. Both eat soft food,
with no or worn-out teeth.
Rocking chair their haven,
the baby is doted on,
rocked and cooed to,
basking in the attention,
while Grandma in the rocker,
provides the power.

A Walk With Elizabeth

Under a fluffy marshmallow sky,
I went for a walk with Elizabeth
who had just turned three,
and what an amazing journey
it turned out to be.

We passed the sidewalk by
and wandered through the garden
toward the cemetery on the hill.
Suddenly we stopped still
and knelt on the garden path
beside the tomato plants,
to watch a persistent little ant
struggle across with a crumb.

Did you know, said Elizabeth,
that is Anty Antaneen,
she's all out of breath,
but she will put that crumb
in a big crumb machine,
cuz she has fourteen babies
in that hole to feed,
and one big crumb is all she needs
to make them stop crying,
and sleep every afternoon
all through August and June.

Oh, and that big black beetle!
See how he hurries around,
his job is strings underneath the ground,
he ties orange strings on carrots,
and red strings on beets
to hold them tight, so they don't
jump out and run away some dark night,
cuz they're afraid we'll eat them
before they get big, big as me almost.

And he puts green strings on beans
so when they lean they won't fall over,
but did you know my thumb can't grow
in my mouth because beetles
can't crawl up my chin or anything
to get in and tie strings
on my teeth, else I'd crunch-
scrunch them all to pieces.

Look at that tater vine,
all dried up in the sun,
goblins were here last night
and around and around they run
and dug taters out of the ground
because taters have eyes
and rutabagers don't.

Did you know worms eat people
when they're dead,
Isn't that scary,
and when robins eat their heads off
worms get false teeth,
that's why they bury a dentist
in every cemetery
that's what Alex said.

And at night trees
bend their branches down
and lean on the ground to rest,
then the rabbits can climb up
and visit the squirrels' nest,
and when a woodpecker
hammers on a tree,
the tree hollers, "Ouch, ouch!!

You're hurting me."
Only you can't hear it,
unless you are standing real near it.

About that time I realized
we should hurry home,
and notify the publishers
to demand an immediate recall
of all scientifically inaccurate
encyclopedias before school starts in fall,
and arrange a consultation
with all supposedly knowledgeable scientists
in the entire nation,
so they can learn the truth and ponder
the amazing information that was all new to me
when I went for a walk with Elizabeth
who had just turned three.

A Louse for Every Hair

Joe came over yesterday to play,
if he stayed outside we coped,
his hair has seldom seen a comb,
his body seldom soaped.
He stayed until the sun went down,
and monsters claimed the dark,
thunder clouds hid moon and stars,
coyotes howled and farm dogs barked.

Then Grandpa told a ghostly tale,
about the shack on knobby hill,
patronized by spirit forms,
who grab folks just for thrills.

Joe was so scared Mama let him stay.
She made his bed on a thick rag rug,
on the kitchen floor, with a rolled up towel
as pillow for his colony of bugs.

Our life went on day after day,
until, a short time later, Mama realized
Joe had left a few guests behind,
but she allowed it was no surprise.

Mama tried to explain the facts
to Joe's Ma, who laughed, "well, I declare,
my Joe's just like our shaggy dog.
He has a louse for every hair."

Saturday Night

After supper the ritual began,
first shift, tangle of littlest kids, frosted with scent
of dog perfume, blended with barn yard mud
hopped in the tub, splashed like playful dolphins,
did the "ouch, ouch" dirty ear wash squirm
captured with towels in mother's or big sister arms.
In went the-age-of-modesty crowd, one by one,
while pajama clad first shift, prayers prayed,
kisses kissed, were tucked in bed.
Boys did the Saturday night slide,
across the newly waxed solid oak floor,
zoomed from kitchen sink, through hallway,
legal end of glide, six inches before
north bedroom window, only once,
a narrow escape, the errant slider saved
from mutilation by the window's heavy drapes.

Girl's Sunday dresses, slips, panties and anklets,
boy's suits, shirts, shorts, socks
segregated on individual hangers,
polished Sunday shoes standing ready
for the dash to arrive at church well before
the bell ringer rang the bell.
Girls hair in bobby-pinned curly-cue strait jackets,
cowlicks brushed out of jostled haired boys.
Mother scrubbed the dirt off Father's back
during his turn for the tub,
then he ate his ice cream and "hit the sack".
All others snuggled in their cocoons.
Finally, Mother got her sub-lukewarm bath
and went into bed confidently prepared
for the Sunday morning dash.

Our Family Car

Every time we go away,
Our Papa gets the Chevrolet,
A host of kids climb in the back,
While the springs and chassis cracks,
Then Mom climbs in her best gown,
And we are set to see the town.

Mom and Pop sit up in front,
And thus escape the wicked brunt,
Of heels and weights that crush the toes,
And arms and backs that poke the nose.
The body bends with what it hauls,
For every time we move at all,
We're stuffed so tight, the poor old bus,
Just has to bend and squirm with us.

We go along a mile or so,
And feel a tire going low,
And every time we hit a hole,
The cushion seems to lose its soul,
While kids that sit on top of us,
Are pounded to unconsciousness.

When people hear us going by,
We never fail to catch their eye,
They stop their work and stare a while,
And we can see them smirk and smile,
For it is worth an actor's pay,
To see our bulging Chevrolet,
When all the kids and Mom and Pop,
Push out the back and sides and top.

Trials of the Firstborn

There are trials in being first,
Some not so bad, some are the worst.
This experience has been mine,
As oldest child in a gang of nine.
When first my parents' job was new,
You'd never guess what I went through!
Was Birdeye, gauze or flannel best?
Did I need a band beneath my chest?
Were egg whites fed, or just the yolks?
Whatever their problem, first my folks
Tried it on me,
Just to see!

Should babies be allowed to cry?
Is nature best, and if so, why?
Are babies rocked, or stuck in bed?
Are tickles best on foot or head?
When children act the little brat,
Should parents settle for a chat?
Or should they spank with seven strokes?
To find the answer, first my folks
Tried it on me,
Just to see!

I saved money to buy a bike,
And when I balked, I had to hike.
But worst of all, in a good old fight,
I could never prove that I was right,
For I was scolded, can't you see?
All the kids were smaller than me!
Mom always said, "You're bigger, dear,"
'Til I sometimes thought they borned me here,
To try things on me,
Just to see!

Now I'm convinced from all these years,
Of having fun despite my tears,
That my four sisters and my four brothers,
Should turn out better than any others,
For I was oldest, and it is no joke,
To solve any problems, first my folks
Tried it on me
Just to see!

The Hair Rebellion

And then there was hair!
Who would have thought
that eagerly awaited fuzz
on baby's charming bald pate
would eventually cause dissension,
despair, total incompatibility
of thought between the generations?

Down,
      Down,
the fuzz grew, past the ears
to the collar and beyond,
and sometimes, in the wind,
past the eyes in wild profusion.

"Oh, God, is this our son,
flesh of our flesh,
our pride, our joy?",
anguished parents wailed,
and though men seldom wept,
fathers sometimes did over hair,
because they looked no further
than length of locks.
It seemed to them
that everything they stood for
had been ripped from the foundations
of their generation.

And shaken by this hairy
assertion of independence,
aunts, uncles, grandparents,
and even righteous neighbor
shook their heads,

ladled out snide remarks,
and young men retreating under
verdant mops, clung more tenacious
to their locks, and kept
the barber eating hamburger.

The statue in front of the church,
overlooking the alter was not called hippy,
nor was great-grandpa, whose portrait
graced the mantle, resplendent with bushy beard
and scraggly locks,
but because his son was so classified,
father, bewildered, in anger and
frustration, disowned his son,
not realizing that while he only
intended to throw out the hair,
he threw out his whole son.

Now when the clouds have rolled away,
and familiarity has bred acceptance,
a new peer group
maneuvers that abundant crop
into some barber's waste basket,
and everything from bald pates
to braids or copious mop-tops
crown those round bowls
of brain cage.

And shaken by this hairy assertion
of independence, fathers, mothers,
aunts, uncles, grandparents,
and even righteous neighbors.

British Columbia Hitchhiker

Wistful eyed stranger,
alone on the long ribbon of road,
teenager ripening into manhood,
young face fresh as the dew
in the first blush of sunrise,
innocent, yet fledgling worldly wise.

My mother heart commanded me
to reward your hesitant thumbing
and gather you up from the highway,
but like a raindrop helplessly falling
the motor home propelled us onward.

Others we passed with no longing,
no tugging of conscience stricken,
but in you I envisioned my son
who walked this very same road -
it was only a summer ago.

After near two hours of miles,
again you appeared from nowhere,
your duffle bag hugging your legs
like a crumpled blue denim puppy
sharing his master's exhaustion.

We stopped this time off the highway,
just ahead on the steep mountain curve,
but you were too long in coming,
my husband's patience too thrifty,
and he powered the motor home onward.

Though I know you will not be stranded,
my heart aches for you, and for me,
for often my conscience will wonder,
who you are and where you are going,
and is a mother's love calling you home?

Corned Sausage

There was flint corn in the sausage,
When I cut it with a knife,
That has never ever happened
In all of my whole life.
Poor Grandma had a kit-fit
When she bit into the corn,
She vowed it never happened
Since the day that she was born.

The kids were in the basement,
When we got the stuffer out,
That explains the reason
This sad story came about.
They were playing with their flint corn,
Down on the basement floor,
They dumped it in the stuffer,
A couple cups or more.

A neighbor ventured over,
And at lunch he took a bite,
He stopped chewin' on his sandwich,
His sunburned face turned white.
Now the neighbors and relation
Don't seem to like the crunch,
For they will drink our coffee,
But won't ever eat our lunch.

Oh, there's flint corn in our sausage,
Blue and red and yellow brown,
It is such a scandal now the story is around,
To the neighbors in the country
And relation in the town,
That there's flint corn in our sausage,
Blue and red and yellow brown.

My Blacksmith Husband

Out to his creaky blacksmith shop,
My darling Hubby goes,
I hear the groaning of the irons,
Beneath his mighty blows.
He turns the crank beside his forge,
To make the fire go,
While in the red hot burning coals
White hot the irons glow.

I know he loves the work he does,
He enjoys every minute,
I am glad that he can find,
A lasting joy in it.
I'll bake a cake for him to eat,
I'll keep the coffee hot,
So my Hubby in the blacksmith shop
Will know he's not forgot.

Death In The Nursing Home

They sit beside the old man's bed,
and strain to ease his labored breath,
blood of his blood, they hold his hands
and sponge his arid lips, and know
that he is dying.

The clergyman now come and gone,
brought consolation and his prayers;
then left to work among the living,
who fantasize that death and sorrow
will wait until a far tomorrow.

Sad children with their father,
they watch and wait, and whisper in
the night. Tickticktock, slowly the
clock of life is winding down, his
time has come, it won't be long.

At last his breathing hesitates,
and at the brink of death, wavers
once, is still, then lay his marbled
hands at rest, at peace the struggle
of his breath.

Looking back for one last time, his
children trudge the dim lit hall
toward home, and sense the shift
of generations, while he rests
in the tranquil hush of death.

III. Seasons

The Seasons

Spring is the delicate bud,
Summer the flower in bloom,
Autumn is the flower dying,
And winter, the snow white tomb.

My Heart Strings Are Tied To The Prairie

My heartstrings are tied to the prairie,
Tied by a rainbow's chain,
Which is only fastened more firmly,
With the hope of the falling rain.
Tied by the creek in the meadow's green,
Where the flowers dance and nod,
Tied by all the beautiful things
That speak to me of God.

The train on the track in the distance,
Resembles a city at night,
Escorted by cars on the highway,
It whistles its way from sight.
The fields of grain in the breezes,
Smiles on a neighbor's face,
The lighted towns for miles around
Make the prairie a friendly place.

The valleys and hills are lonely,
With trees that tower on high,
Just give me a home on the prairie
To love 'til the day I die,
For my heartstrings are tied with
a rainbow's chain
To the prairie, wide open and free,
Though others may leave it for places afar,
It's home, sweet home to me.

The Emissaries

Black is the night and the wind
moans around in the dark,
and makes a soulful sound.
Soft as a lullaby song
hums the rain on the roof,
and wets the waiting ground.
Clouds in a mass, while the moon,
far above in the sky,
is hidden away from sight.
Geese on their way from the south,
proclaim the welcome tidings
that spring has come tonight.

Summer's Song

The sound of running feet
of little girls and boys,
singing summer's song,
an exuberance of joy.

Kites and balls and each other
they come running after,
blending with the grass and flowers,
with melodies of laughter.

I listen to their happy play,
standing at the door,
and in my imagination,
I become a child once more.

To skip across a grassy lawn,
and play the whole day long,
remembering the time long gone,
when I, too, sang summer's song.

Morning Meditations

Twining a maze of blue,
high up on the yard light pole,
weaving a tapestry
obedient to the sun,
the morning glories
welcome the day,
earthly reflections
of morning's blue skies.

Metamorphosis

"I am Man's Knowledge,"
I said to the stars,
flashing in obedient patterns
across the heavens.
"I know all things.
Listen to me!
How foolish your dreams
to dazzle the earth forever,
already a blanket of smog
hides the infinite sky."

"And as for you,
planet of borrowed light,
no longer sliver king
of foolish hearts,
satellite of dust and rock,
how dare you sift dust
over man's footprints
and his abandoned capsules,
his knowledge has ruled you.
Listen to me!"
But, programmed from creation,
their course never altered.

I tried to imprison
pregnant seeds and sleeping roots,
buried so long beneath the snow.
"Why stir from dormant beds,
when earth entices with false hope,
and death is the end of it all?
Listen to me!" I said.
But they flaunted
the seed of harvest in my face.

I tried in vain to smother
the burning flame of love,
this consuming passion
would surely end in sorrow.
"Listen to me!" I said.
But love conquered the atom,
and is still burping with joy.

"Foolish birds,"
I said, in the spring,
"Forcing eager wings in frantic endeavor,
building nests from scattered bits
of straw and string,
weaving imprudent hopes
of flagrant reproduction.
Are you ignorant of Man's Knowledge?
Listen to me, I know all things!
The earth trembles with fear,
all is futile!"
But their song never faltered.

Nothing would attune its ear
to Man's Knowledge.
Humanity's burdens ravaged my senses,
and confusion hung over the earth.
A great chasm of emptiness
terrified me, and I wept
long seasons of darkness.

Then the Word consumed me,
The Light burned, and was blinding.
The heat from the fire purified my Ego;

I struggled in defiance
as He molded me,
until I lay, molded, in ashes.

I was Man's Knowledge,
I was nothing,
Now I am Wisdom.

Norfolk

Norfolk, nestled in Elkhorn valley,
Bustling with life and living,
City of factories and schools,
Rich in apartments and houses,
And restaurants that beckon the hungry,
Gratifiers of selective taste buds,
From ordinary to elitist gourmet.

Tall corn waving in wind gusts,
Rustle green leaves at her boundaries,
While the Elkhorn, rampaging or gentle,
Outlines Tahazouka's south edges,
Where families picnic in season,
Serenaded with wild bird songs.

At Fourth of July celebrations,
Kaleidoscopic the skies of evening,
Bursting with fireworks flashing
Reflected in Skyview Lake,
While the crowded lake slopes tremble,
With echoes like cannon shots sounding,
Other times fishermen gather
To sink their fresh baited hooks,
In the long lake's placid waters.

Norfolk, city of molten steel,
Channel for livestock and grain,
Manufacturer for world demand,
Haven for the sick and weary,
Where sanctuaries chime their carillons,
And shepherd faith hungry souls.

Home of the arts, and of music,
Cradle of talented stars,
Norfolk, our smorgasbord city.
Blinking with a blanket of lights,
Across the valley at nighttime,
Sleeping, yet awake in the shadows,
Holding us secure in her bosom,
Loyal to our heart's devotion,
Norfolk, our sovereign city,
The place we proudly call home.

Thanksgiving

We traveled while summer
was building the harvest,
along our journeyed way
the scorching sun shone hot,
the scathing winds blew dry,
while thirsty fields were browned
by relentless drought,
not harvest's golden hue.

How humbling to return
to lush fields, summer green,
where each time the land
would open up parched lips,
heaven's overflowing urn
poured ample rain, to seal
a partnership with earth,
to bring forth abundance.

Want and plenty abide
together, where life is.
Man plants the seed, aware,
God sends either harvest,
or brown and barren fields;
with empty bins and want,
God also sends eternal hope
for another season.

Country

Country,
no other word
so many lovely visions wake
as country.
Songbirds flash their prismy patterns
across a leaf splashed sky, and sing
their never ending symphonies
in harmony with violins of cottonwood
and oak, and the woodpecker's
loud staccato on his drum.

Country,
a sometimes paradise.
Satin breezes ripple emerald
plains of grass: sunshine tames
the wild rain and kisses rolling
meadowlands where cattle, grazing,
needle random stitches, red, white,
and black, across green valleyed
tapestries, tree hung from summer skies.

Country,
kaleidoscope of elements.
Capricious winter's maverick blizzards
immobilize all life: isolation's
snowbound silence reclaims peace.
Summer's tornadic violence
may devastate the land, yet from
the rainbow's urn of promise
country people drink of courage
and of hope, still believing
no other word
so many lovely visions wake
as country.

The Unveiling

The leaves are gone from the bushes,
The weeds are all gone from the fence,
No longer is our vision obstructed.
By foliage, both fragrant and dense;
Our freedom is gone with the summer,
Our labors are hidden no more,
So now when the urge overtakes us,
We must close up the outhouse door.

A Matter of Necessity

I'm just an old building,
With cracks in the wall,
I'm not a nice thing
To look at all;
I creak and I bend,
I let in the storm,
My abode in the winter
Is not at all warm.
So it's not for these things,
Folks patronize me,
But for the two holes,
They sit on, I see.

Gasless Get-About

When my Camaro crashed last fall,
I spurned the local dealer's call,
then to my four-wheeled friends surprise,
a prancing filly met their eyes.

Trans Am, Corvettes, of such they brag,
and taunt my horse, "that clumsy nag."
but as they beep, and whiz on by,
I glimpse an envy in their eye,
for while they pump three dollar gas,
my barn is full of natural grass.

The Tree Trimmers

It is I, only I
who weeps for my maples
as the roar of chain saws
shatters the morning quiet,
sputtering, reviving, chains whirring
slicing superfluous branches
denuding sinewy trunks
on copious maples grown shaggy.

It is only I who stands here weeping,
watching leaf fingered twigs
cling like rejected lovers
as severed branches fall,
until, green on the withered brown lawn,
gross carnage fractures the circle
of maple tree shade.

It is only I
who weeps for my maples
standing half naked and wounded,
their wind songs plundered by tree trimmers,
tree trimmers who walk away whistling
their stolen songs.

The Robin and the Worm

If I were a worm
in a robin's beak,
I would wiggle and squirm,
and tweak his cheek,
I would stare in his eye,
and then I would say,
"Put me down and go eat
some other bug today,
because if you swallow me
I'll swell round as a cup,
and make you so miserable
you'll have to cough me up."

Daffodils

I placed the silken daffodils on the sofa table,
and vision yellow seas across the greening hills
in spring, my medicine to survive the winter.

Before the Roses Bloom

Before the roses bloom,
before the fields turn green
and calves follow the cow to pasture,
silky coats shining in the sun.
Before five buckle overshoes
are washed clean and rest in the shop,
and snorting tractors quit
plowing furrows across the yards,
the snow melts, and the season
of mud comes, clay mud that sucks down,
like a powerful vacuum cleaner
sucks down small children,
Rescued by mothers plugging out
Pulling up wailing children,
encased in plaster casts of clay,
tugging their rubber boots
before they get to China.

Autumn Leaves

Autumn leaves
   Suspended,
Bright confetti
   Swirling,
Hang-gliding
   Gold-red silhouettes
Aloft
   in wind-blown skies.

Go Go Little Birds

The weatherman predicts
hard frost tonight, I gather sticks
for the winter bitter;
flocks of birds all a-twitter
in scarlet leaves of maple trees,
apparently have heard the dire news
and now must chose to start
their southerly flight.

Go, go, little birds,
before autumn's fickle glory
turns to white, or else endure
the bitter winter with me.
I shall sit before a blazing fire,
and wrap in blankets soft and warm,
while you will cling to brittle branches
of naked maple trees, and freeze in cold
and storm and most certainly expire.

Go, go, little birds
do not take such foolish chances,
be not deceived by scarlet leaves
that tempt you to tarry here,
do not believe their cloak
will shield you, they linger
such brief hours, and soon will weave
your scarlet bier on faded flowers

Go, go, little birds,
before the cold winds blow,
go claim the sanctuary
of far lands alien to snow.

The Believers

Flash of red cap,
and white-throated belly,
pink breasted dove,
red breasted robin,
and drab little wren,
fleet shadows darting
past my big window,
beaks grasping grass,
an odd straw or string,
for building their nests,
never minding a tish,
the wren house hangs
at precarious angles
from half-broken branches.

None of them fret
the yard trees are dead,
as they flit to and fro,
purposely building,
never once doubting
the world goes on,
and instinctive routines
will last forever.

The Lord must cherish
such believers.

Little Green Apples

Little green apples, newly born,
Green as the green of leaves they adorn,
Bathed in the mist of dawn's fog sea,
Rocked in the arms of the apple tree.

Mother in June, pink-blossomed in May,
Babies replacing her bridal array,
Safe on her breast her little ones lie,
Rocked in her arms as the wind goes by.

Fisherman's Delight

I feel the creepy wiggle worm,
rebelling, twist and bend and squirm,
while I, with thoughtless ecstasy,
so quickly end his destiny.

The baited hook becomes a part
of lapping waves, my drowsy eyes
ever on the bobber, floating
and darting in reflected skies.
I dream, and swat the buzzing flies,
and sip contentment's pure delight,
completely taken by surprise,
when fish are prone to take a bite.

The moment that the bobber dives
beneath the waves, I jerk the pole.
A silver flash like dew at dawn,
whose fins and tail have lost control
of motion, lands upon the shore.
I cast again into the shoal,
twice blest, as God renews my store
of food for body, food for soul.

Roz And Rosalie

In August, Roz and Rosy came to stay,
we loved them from the very first day.
They did not bite or scratch at all,
they were the sweetest, purring balls
of fluffy fur, who loved to play -
we wouldn't give these kitties away!

Then we discovered Roz and Rosy gone,
we looked everywhere, under, over, on.
Our friend across the street had news,
it wasn't good, it gave us blues,
a dumpy woman in a black sedan,
apparently had a well-laid plan.

As soon as we drove down the street -
she was not even that discreet -
She parked at the end of our driveway,
ran up, where the kittens loved to play,
grabbed Roz and Rosy to our dismay,
under her coat to the black sedan,
to her kitty cage, fast she ran,
thrust them in, in quite a hurry,
speeded off, leaving us to worry
where and why our kitties are gone.

We know we should say, "Father, forgive,"
we know it is the proper way to live,
but she had planned what she would do,
she knew what she was doing, she knew.
Couldn't we wish on her horrid dreams,
of cats chasing her with laser beams,
lion size cats, anytime she went to bed
that would yowl around inside her head?

Silly Milly Ran Away

A silly filly, name of Milly,
Ran away one summer night.
She galloped fast across the meadow,
Found her freedom such delight.
Until she tumbled in a gully,
In the dark, quite out of sight,
And sliding to the rocky bottom,
Trembled, quivered, faint with fright.

Plunging through the thistle thorns
And prickly weeds, all growing there,
She soon had zillion things attached
To her groomed and shining hair.
They latched unto her flowing mane,
And clustered on her tail,
They prickled deep her tender hide,
Poor Milly's heart began to quail.

Her ears perked up, her heart beat wild,
As foxes yipped, and badgers prowled,
While field mice scurried through the weeds,
And in the hills coyotes howled.
She shivered in the dark and cold,
As showers spattered from the sky,
She wished she'd never run away,
And cried a mournful filly cry.

She cried throughout the horrid night
And morning brought its own dismay,
She feared no one would ever find her,
Even in the light of day.
The summer sun burned on her back,
Suffocating soared the heat,
There was no water there to drink,
Not a spear of grass to eat.

The ugly buzzards circled low,
The stinkbugs labored on the banks,
Lizzards scurried under rocks,
While gadflies nibbled at her flanks.
Then distant in the muggy heat,
A roaring muffled sound she heard,
Which coming closer proved to be,
A monstrous whirling Whirlybird.

Windy Whirly whirred above her,
It fanned the dust into her eyes,
Soon a man and rope were lowered,
Help was coming from the skies!
He tied a canvas around her belly,
Tied her in it, snuggled tight,
They lifted her right out the gully,
Where she had spent the horrid night.

Up and up, the Whirly whirred,
Taking Milly for a ride,
High above the dusty gully,
The hills and meadows, miles wide.
Worried Mama in the barnyard,
Ran to greet her little filly,
"I'll never, ever run away,"
Promptly vowed a wiser Milly.

Little Mouse In My House

Little mouse in my house,
How thoughtless to construct your nest,
and expect to be my welcome guest.
If I should intrude in a lion's den,
do you think they would pretend
I was a lion, and welcome me to the pride?
I fear I would be forced to hide.
After all, I am not a Daniel.

I warn you, little mouse in my house,
I shall consider you as the lion in his lair
would consider me, wallow in despair,
for I will set traps, although I won't eat you,
tasty morsels will greet you
in unexpected places, and they will not be cheese,
but will close your beady eyes by sneaky degrees.

Be advised, little mouse in my house,
Either leave my premises or quake with fear,
for I will know if you are still here,
by all the tidbits you leave behind,
plus a human always knows wherever a mouse goes
by the offensive attack on his nose
so if you are wise you will quickly find
a more suitable abode
farther on down the road.
Should I be more considerate than a lion?

Renaissance Romance

An ill-advised swain named Hans,
Indulged in forbidden romance,
He took her red roses,
And died one supposes,
On the very sharp end of a lance.

One Question, Please

Man evolved from monkeys,
Darwin's theory does insist,
But I cannot help but wonder,
Why the monkeys still exist.

Mistaken Calendar

The calendar says spring,
I don't think it's right,
For even through it's May Day,
I'm still flanneled at night.

Line Dance

Frozen sheets dance in line,
stiff as arthritic grandmothers,
gradually at the wind's urging
movements become more supple,
and they dance with rhythmic abandon,
forgetting their morning of stiffness.

At evening I smooth them on my bed,
my joints loosened from a day's slow
dancing at mundane tasks, I snuggle down
in their softness to rest my weary bones.

Prairie Song

A half-century Nebraska hills
have sheltered me,
yet no matter where I roam,
my child heart claims Dakota
plains as home. When I return
I thrill at vast expanse
of flat land wide as sky,
the familiar trill of meadowlark,
the song of turtle dove.
And when the busy day
is done, I open wide my
window to welcome
an especially remembered love,
the wind that evening brings,
the wind that sings the prairie's
song on summer nights.

The night wind feathers
coolness across my face,
whispers memories of long ago,
memories of scalding sun,
of suffocating heat, and day winds
burning crops that failed to grow;
memories of waiting for night
to come, to spread its mantle
over the land, when prairie winds
would cool the ravages of long hot
days, its touch like angel hands.

I have traveled over mountains
and through valleys in the glory
of their splendid best; I have
stumbled over rough terrain,
and stood on the beach in rain,
yet only the plains are balm
for my heart's unrest.

There, though changes master
the horizon, this special
remembering is my delight,
this knowing, that sure
as a mother hums her lullabies
to quiet her fretful child,
the Creator will always send
the wind at evening, to sing
the prairie's song on summer nights.

The Prairie Pines

My heartstrings are tied to the prairie,
to the prairie, wide open and free,
Where water waves and the sun shines,
and bulls bellow, and the wind whines,
Where buffalos bunch, and the mud mires,
and lowlands level, and hills higher,
Where deer dash, and fawns flee,
and coons cuddle, and sandbars squeeze,
Where rains gush, and ducks dine,
and willows weep, while the prairie pines.

Victory

The nurse unwound the blood pressure cuff
from his bone arm, and turned away
from the anguished hunger in his eyes,
the waiting for death hunger.

They had tried, meaning a round of doctors,
in a round of clinics and hospitals,
with surgery, and chemo, diet and laughter,
but the enemy eluded them, like guerillas

imbedded in the jungle, stealthy
and ready to attack, and no one knew
what cell the enemy was hiding in
or where it would strike again.

The nurse checked the needle in his hand
the glucose dripped in his vein,
feeding him, at the same time nourishing
that thing that gnawed away inside.

Down the street the church bells tolled,
and he whispered through lips parched
as dry earth in prairie drought,
"toll for me, toll for me."

"What time is it?" he asked the nurse.
"Twenty minutes after nine," she said.
A heavenly quiet filled the room,
with joyous hallelujahs his soul

leaped free; at last that insidious thing,
inside of him, relentless parasite
that could not be conquered in life
would also die - death was his victory!

When Death Comes

When death comes, we ponder
without understanding,
submissive to the fear that
awakens within us.
With sad and whispered voices,
we yield our human will,
to that power which the Lord has
to govern life and death,
- tis then possessions keep no
stronghold in our hearts.

When the coffin lies an earthy
mound, and the shovel rests,
and funeral flowers are memories
pressed in laid away books,
too soon we all forget, and back
along the same old road,
again we make our way,
forgetting we have an end,
to bicker over small things, and busy
our minds with much doing,
wasting life's precious hours, as if
masters of our souls;
may our lamps be burning bright
when the night comes.

Life's Setting Sun

Life's sunset with its parting is at our shadowed door,
Vacant is our father's chair, his face we'll see no more.
Twilight's sweat of agony no longer beads his brow,
Safe within his Savior's arms his soul is resting now.

We who watched him suffer out his last long hours of pain,
Could not wish that he were back, to suffer and weep again,
Yet, Lord, sustain our grieving hearts, our father dear is gone,
Our darkest hour has brought him to Thy eternal dawn.

This earth's shadowed night must be before the sun can rise,
No darkness intervenes for him who sees eternal skies;
Night's darkest hours belong to us, who here must watch him go,
Heaven's dawn for him, as yet, we mortals cannot know.

Though our hearts are rent and torn with grief,
God knows what is best,
Until we meet again, dear Lord, give to him sweet rest.

Meditation

I gaze out the window
at the moon,
lonesome light
in midnight sky,
peeking through gaps
in clouds floating by,
hiding the stars.
Placid moon,
confident that the stars
still shine.

Flesh lives out its brief time,
and turns to dust,
same old moon shines on,
through ages and ages
plies its set course,
and lights the soul's way home.

When the Master Calls

Soon glistens the light of the rising sun,
On the green hills damp with the dew,
While the breeze still sleeps
in the veil of the mist,
That covers the hill and the slough.

The white-faced steers in the quietness stir,
To graze on the sides of the hill,
Till a voice rings out with a call
through the dawn,
And the life that is awakened is still,
And deep is the hush as they stop in the grass,
Then the steers raise their white heads high,
And the quiet is broken as they answer him back,
For their master has sounded his cry.

Then again comes the call to beckon them home,
And slowly they start, then faster,
Till the morning is filled with the trample of hooves
As they run at the call of their master.
And the picture is like to the dawn of our night,
In the valley of the mist we'll roam,
And we'll answer with joy at the sound of his voice,
When our Master is calling us home.

Plea Bargain

Please wait, Jack Frost, cancel your
appointment with September. Late October
will grant you ample time to sentence
autumn's loveliness to death. Do not

distress my delicate impatiens, my
delphiniums and dahlias blooming late,
my climbing roses twining vibrant rainbows
above the trellised gate, and lush tomatoes
pinked on optimistic vines. Wait until

the farmers gather in their soybeans and
maize, matured and ready for the bin.
Spare my pumpkins glowing orange in
autumn's sun. Let them linger long through
golden laze of Indian Summer, before
they feel the chill your icy fingers bring.

Please, Jack Frost, this is my plea,
I believe it only fair, since you have
had your way these many years, to grant
this just reprieve, and spare this rare
and glorious autumn especially for me.

About the Author

Dorthy Knouse Koepke, poet, author, and speaker, was born in 1922, in Kingsbury County, South Dakota, the oldest girl in a family of nine children. She was raised in South Dakota and began writing when she was 12 years old. Her first poem was published when she was only 16. She finished eighth grade in 1935 and spent the next three years at home caring for her younger siblings. At age16, she began High School in Cavour, South Dakota, while working for a couple for room and board. Through this couple she met her future husband.

In 1942, she graduated High School as valedictorian. She attended Huron College for one year and majored in journalism. Dorthy was assistant editor of the college paper and secretary-treasurer of her sorority, Pi Alpha Phi. Although she received two scholarships to attend college, she had to work a variety of jobs to make ends meet. Two such jobs included washing dishes at the bus stop for twenty-five cents an hour, and writing several features for the Evening *Huronite* newspaper. In 1990, she was named Alumnus of the Month by Huron University in Huron, South Dakota.

Dorthy married Herman in 1943, and moved to Hoskins, Nebraska. Raising ten kids kept her too busy to become worldly famous but gave her more than enough inspiration and ideas for writing fodder, from which she created hundreds of poems and stories.

In addition to writing, she listed her occupations as Manager & Bookkeeper for the Koepke Farm, and Enthusiastic Mother of Ten Children.

She has written, published, and received numerous honors and awards in local and national venues for many of her poems and short stories. A poem "Dust Bowl," won first place in a national contest and received praise from Bill Kloefkorn, State Poet of Nebraska, who once called it "an example of a perfect poem."

She has also written a children's book, which is yet unpublished.

She satisfied her desire to return to school by attending writer's workshops, seminars and conferences. Many times, day and night, healthy or sick, washing clothes or dishes, cooking mountains of food, tending children, husband, and relatives, or milking cows, she would be reciting poetry, or stopping all of a sudden to quick jot down a note or idea, or write a new poem just composed in her mind. She squeezed in writing time at her desk and typewriter in the "study," which often was just a bedroom with several beds, a crib, and a dresser.

Her poetry is an intimate look at her thoughts and feelings as a farm wife, mother and faithful disciple of God. She gives some of the credit for her writing abilities to her grandmother who hailed from York, England, and was a storyteller with a keen sense of humor.

She is a member of the Spindrift Poets Club in Norfolk, Nebraska, as well as the Nebraska Chaparral Poets, of which she has served on the executive board. She has been a member of the National Writers Club and the Society of Children's book writers.

Her work has been published in *Midwest Living Magazine, Highlights for Children, Christian Science Monitor, Guidepost Magazine, Magazine of the Midlands, Grit Magazine, Whole Notes, Midwest Poetry Review, National Writer's Club, This Day Magazine, Nebraska Center for the Book, Lutheran Witness, Celebrate - University of Nebraska-Omaha,* and *South Dakota State Poetry Society - Pasque Petals.*

In 1996, she traveled to Anaheim, California, at the invitation of the Famous Poets Society, to read her poem, "Resurrection" at the Famous Poets Convention.

In 2002, she received first place in the Nebraska Mother's Association and the Mother's Association, Inc., in the essay division of the literature contest with her story "The Real Christmas."

Dorthy's previous books include *Close To My Heart* and *Love Made Me Do It*.

LaVergne, TN USA
04 February 2011
215175LV00003B/8/P